SpringerBriefs in Information Systems

Series editor

Jörg Becker

More information about this series at http://www.springer.com/series/10189

Alexander Hütter · Thomas Arnitz
René Riedl

On the Nature of Effective CIO/CEO Communication

Evidence from an Interview Study

 Springer

Alexander Hütter
Department of Business Informatics
Johannes Kepler University Linz
Linz
Austria

Thomas Arnitz
Department of Business Informatics
Johannes Kepler University Linz
Linz
Austria

René Riedl
University of Applied Sciences Upper
  Austria
Steyr, Oberösterreich
Austria

and

Department of Business Informatics
Johannes Kepler University Linz
Linz
Austria

ISSN 2192-4929   ISSN 2192-4937   (electronic)
SpringerBriefs in Information Systems
ISBN 978-3-319-50534-3   ISBN 978-3-319-50535-0   (eBook)
DOI 10.1007/978-3-319-50535-0

Library of Congress Control Number: 2016960560

Printed on acid-free paper

This Springer imprint is published by Springer Nature
The registered company is Springer International Publishing AG
The registered company address is: Gewerbestrasse 11, 6330 Cham, Switzerland

Contents

On the Nature of Effective CIO/CEO Communication: Evidence from an Interview Study

1 Introduction

Effective communication between the chief information officer (CIO) and chief executive officer (CEO) is critical for both parties to achieve a shared understanding of the role of information technology (IT) in their organization [27, 49, 58, 68]. A shared CIO/CEO understanding of the role of IT is important because it facilitates CIOs obtaining their business peers' commitment for strategic IT initiatives [16, 47]. Further, a shared CIO/CEO understanding improves the alignment of IT and business objectives [29, 53], which, in turn, is positively related to IT and business performance [8].

Despite this importance of effective CIO/CEO communication for organizational IT success, studies frequently report that CIOs and CEOs often have troubles in their communication; hence, misunderstandings about the role of IT exist [24, 67]. There are different reasons for this situation. CEOs and other top managers often state that their CIOs lack the ability to explain IT issues in business terms, and that they tend to use technical jargon that is not readily understood by those outside the IT domain [31, 75]. In contrast, CIOs complain that their business peers misunderstand the value and capabilities of IT, and are often unaware of how IT can be used to support business objectives [36]. Such discrepancies limit CIOs' ability to work effectively with their CEOs in order to meet strategic objectives and derive IT benefits [1].

Only a few scientific studies have investigated explicitly how CIOs and CEOs can achieve effectiveness in their communication. Those studies that focus on CIO/CEO communication effectiveness almost exclusively derived their results from survey data (in English speaking countries), or are conceptual in nature (for details, see Sect. 2). A major reason for the dearth of qualitative research, particularly interviews, could be the difficulty of getting access to, and meaningful data from, busy top managers [65].

© The Author(s) 2017
A. Hütter et al., *On the Nature of Effective CIO/CEO Communication*,
SpringerBriefs in Information Systems, DOI 10.1007/978-3-319-50535-0_1

Communication and shared understanding of IT are two elusive concepts, not easily amenable by the dominant IS research method (i.e., survey) [60]. Moreover, given the relative paucity of qualitative studies on CIO/CEO communication, we decided to conduct an interview study with twelve pairs of CIOs and CEOs in the German-speaking area, more specifically, in Austria (for details, see Sect. 3). Based on this approach, we develop new insight into the nature of CIO/CEO communication effectiveness.

The remainder of this paper is structured as follows: In the next section, we outline theoretical background information on CIO/CEO communication. Specifically, we discuss related work and outline our research model. A discussion of our research methodology follows. Afterward, we present the results. This is followed by a reflection on the results, which may, particularly for practitioners, help in future decisions and actions to cope with challenges related to CIO/CEO communication. Finally, we discuss important implications of our work, as well as limitations, and outline possible avenues for future research.

2 Theoretical Background

2.1 Related Work

The literature on communication competence examines how individuals can achieve both appropriateness and effectiveness in their interactions [6, 14, 18, 43, 46, 64]. Despite the variety of approaches and perspectives that researchers have adopted in communication research, there are three basic elements of communication competence that are discussed as important, namely cognitive knowledge, performance, and motivation [57]. Cognitive knowledge is the knowledge about the subject matter and its corresponding context, as well as the knowledge of how to communicate appropriately and effectively. Performance refers to the interaction partners' actual communication behaviors. Motivation is the incentive of communicators to transfer their cognitive knowledge into the behaviors they actually perform. Based on this insight from the communication competence literature, IS scholars applied a number of theories related to communication to explain effectivity in CIO/CEO communication. Table 1 summarizes related work in chronological order.

From a theoretical perspective, Table 1 shows that Lind and Zmud [41] and Johnson and Lederer [27, 28] used Rogers and Kincaid's [62] convergence model to argue that through cycles of information exchange, the CIO and CEO move toward a mutual understanding of each other's opinion, and thus, create consensus on the organization's role of IT. In addition, both studies have also applied Daft and Lengel's [12] media richness theory to explain the effects of communication channel on CIO/CEO convergence regarding IT's role for business activities.

Lind and Zmud [41] found that more frequent and channel rich communication predicts convergence between technology providers and users regarding the potential of IT to innovatively support business activities. Johnson and Lederer [27, 28]

Table 1 Related work in the IS literature on CIO/CEO communication

Publication	Method	Sample	Country of investigation	Applied theory related to communication	Abstract/major findings
Watson [74]	Survey	43 IS managers	Australia	Media richness [12]	This paper investigates the information scanning behavior of IS executives and the relationship with their CEOs. Based on survey data, the authors report that IS executives who have two-way communication with their CEOs rate IT strategic planning as less critical and that IS executives tend to scan sources that are close to their industry.
Lind and Zmud [41]	Case study	2 divisions from one company	United States	Convergence [62], media richness [12]	This paper examines if a convergence in understanding between providers and users of a technology results in greater innovativeness regarding that technology. The results of this case study indicate that convergence is a predictor of innovativeness, communication richness is a predictor of convergence, and communication frequency is a predictor of both convergence and communication richness.
Stephens and Loughman [68]	Case study	5 CIOs from five companies	United States	No specific theory from communication research	CIOs must be able to communicate complex issues clearly, without overusing technical jargon, to their top management and business unit managers who are often outside the IS function. Based on both quantitative and qualitative data, the paper presents how CIOs conveyed ideas effectively and powerfully to a variety of functional managers.

(continued)

Table 1 (continued)

Publication	Method	Sample	Country of investigation	Applied theory related to communication	Abstract/major findings
Reich and Benbasat [58]	Case study	10 business units from three companies	Canada	No specific theory from communication research	Alignment between IT and organizational objectives is one of the key concerns of IS executives. Thus, this paper investigated, based on a conceptual model, factors that may potentially influence alignment. Results indicate that shared domain knowledge, IT implementation success, communication between business and IT executives, and connections between business and IT planning influence short-term alignment. Only shared domain knowledge was found to influence long-term alignment.
Rattanasampan and Chaidaroon [57]	Conceptual	Not applicable	Not applicable	Communication competence [14]	A relationship between the CIO and business units is important because the implementation and use of IT demands collaborations. This paper proposes that, to improve CIOs' relationships with others and the effectiveness of CIOs' communication, CIOs must possess communication competence (i.e., knowing what, how, and why to communicate).
Preston and Karahanna [52]	Survey	382 CIOs	United States	No specific theory from communication research	This paper examines the development of shared mental models between the CIO and top management about the role of IT in the organization. Based on a model spanning the dimensions of shared language and shared understanding, the paper indicates that relational similarity and formal mechanisms of knowledge exchange (e.g., the CIO hierarchical level) are important to the development of shared mental models.

(continued)

Table 1 (continued)

Publication	Method	Sample	Country of investigation	Applied theory related to communication	Abstract/major findings
Preston et al. [54]	Survey	44 French CIOs, 163 United States CIOs	France, United States	No specific theory from communication research	The development of a shared understanding between the CIO and top managers about the role of IT in the organization is important for achieving IT success. The paper proposes that CIO educational mechanisms impact the development of this shared understanding in both samples. However, while in the French sample social systems of knowing are key mechanisms, in the U.S. sample structural systems of knowing and relational similarity are key mechanisms for achieving a shared understanding.
Johnson and Lederer [27, 28]	Survey	202 CIO/CEO pairs	United States	Convergence [62], media richness [12]	Convergence between an organization's CIO and CEO about the IT is critical for exploiting technology successfully. Supported by communication theory, the paper indicates that more frequent communication leads to convergence about the current role of IT. Convergence about the current role of IT predicted higher IS financial contribution.
Preston and Karahanna [53]	Survey	243 matched-pair CIOs and top managers	United States	No specific theory from communication research	This paper presents a model for creating a shared vision between an organization's CIO and other top managers about the role of IT. Based on survey data, the paper describes how such a shared vision can be facilitated by six visioning mechanisms. Moreover, the paper indicates that a shared IT vision is the key for aligning the organization's IT strategy with its business strategy.

indicate that more frequent communication between the CIO and CEO, as well as the use of richer communication channels in their interactions, predict convergence of opinion about the role of IT in an organization. Moreover, Reich and Benbasat [58] indicate that direct and frequent communication between business executives and IT executives positively influences the level of alignment between IT and business objectives. Watson [74] and Stephens and Loughman [68] point out that richer communication channels provide IT executives with the capacity to communicate strategic IT planning requirements more appropriately to their CEOs, and therefore help IT executives to minimize the complexity of the planning task.

Preston and Karahanna [52, 53] and Preston et al. [54] showed that CIOs who are competent communicators are more effective in creating a shared IT vision and knowledge around the issue of IT-business alignment within an organization's top management than CIOs who are less competent communicators. Furthermore, Rattanasampan and Chaidaroon [57] indicate that effective communication qualifies CIOs to establish executive working relationships and collaborations across department boundaries. These executive relationships, in turn, make it easier for CIOs to gain their CEOs commitment for organization-wide IT changes, and collaborations with others pave the way for implementing those changes successfully.

From a methodological perspective, five facts are important to note (see Table 1). First, survey, and hence quantitative research, is the dominant methodological approach. Second, it follows that qualitative research is less common. Third, qualitative research was carried out in the form of case studies, but not in the form of paired interviews with CIOs and CEOs within organizations, which could also provide deep insights into CIO/CEO communication. Fourth, qualitative research was carried out only in the early period of CIO/CEO communication research (we were not able to identify qualitative research in the last 15 years). Fifth, most studies were conducted in English speaking countries. Hence, there is a paucity of research in other geographical areas.

To sum up, the current IS research stream has a narrow focus on communication frequency and communication channels in describing how CIOs and CEOs can achieve effectiveness in their interactions. To advance knowledge in this research area and to close research gaps surrounding effective CIO/CEO communication, we developed an a priori research model which served as a basis for our interview study.

2.2   Research Model

Based on the related work (see Sect. 2.1) and further CIO literature (identified through a systematic literature review; the entire list of CIO papers is available by request), we developed an initial model for investigating effective CIO/CEO communication. Specifically, to extend the insights reported in the related work on CIO/CEO communication (Table 1), we reviewed the CIO literature for additional factors and relationships that are currently not addressed in the context of effective CIO/CEO communication, but are potentially important for understanding its antecedents and consequences. Based on this additional analysis, we identified, in addition to communication frequency and communication channel, communication content, communication style, personal characteristics, and CIO hierarchical position as important for effective CIO/CEO communication. Figure 1 shows our research model. In the following subsections, we detail the factors and relationships.

CIO Hierarchical Position. CIO hierarchical position is defined as the organizational rank and status of the CIO that enables him/her to communicate with the CEO about IT themes [32]. A high hierarchical position provides the CIO with opportunities for official engagements with the CEO (see the upper echelons theory [21]) and increases the nature and level of their IT interactions [2, 40]. Further, a high hierarchical position can strengthen CIO authority and power [17, 66]. Higher levels of engagements between the CIO and CEO may provide the CIO with a greater understanding of the organization's business practices, goals, and visions [2, 15]. These engagements also offer a potential forum for the CEO to learn about the capabilities of IT and how IT can be employed to support the business strategy and value-chain activities [70].

CIO/CEO Communication Frequency. Communication frequency describes how often an organization's CIO and CEO communicate about IT themes. Frequency of communication enables both executives to develop common definitions of situations, reduce barriers, and build consensus [58, 71]. Frequent CIO/CEO communication about IT themes predicts greater convergence in their views of the role of IT in their organization and its expected contribution to the business [27, 41]. Regular discussions also help both executives to share information which is strategically important to the organization and thus positively influences a CEO's view of IT [2, 26].

CIO/CEO Communication Channel Naturalness. Communication channel naturalness is defined as the naturalness of a medium that is used by an organization's CIO and CEO to communicate about IT themes. Prior research has often

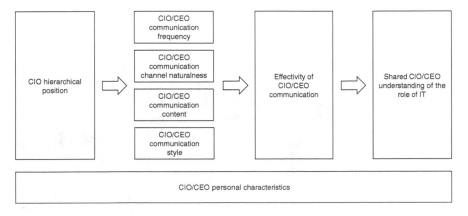

Fig. 1 A priori research model

used Daft and Lengel's [12] media richness theory to examine the impact of communication channels on outcome variables [13]. However, Kock [37] derived a new theory from evolutionary psychology theorizing proposing that the naturalness of a medium is more important than its richness. Specifically, in his media naturalness theory he proposes that a decrease in the degree of naturalness results in three major effects regarding a communication process: (1) increased cognitive effort, (2) increased ambiguity, and (3) decreased physiological arousal in terms of excitement [38].[1] However, achieving a shared CIO/CEO understanding of the role of IT is a difficult process (implying reciprocal understanding of emotions, intentions, and reasoning processes), and thus, following Kock's theory, more natural communication channels (ideally face-to-face) will impact the nature of CIO/CEO communication.

CIO/CEO Communication Content. Communication content comprises the IT themes which are discussed by an organization's CIO and CEO during their meetings. The type of themes discussed by an organization's CIO and CEO plays a key role in developing a shared understanding of the role of IT in the organization [1, 40]. CIOs who communicate mainly about strategic IT themes with their business peers (e.g., when the CIO and CEO discuss an IT strategy instead of how a module of the enterprise resource planning (ERP) system supports a specific business process) are more effective in providing them with the appropriate perspective on how to align IT with organizational structures and goals [36, 42]. A strategic discussion of IT themes ensures that business and IT capabilities are integrated into technical solutions that support the organization effectively [61, 63]. These discussions also allow for the transfer of business and IT knowledge between the CIO and CEO, and ensure that the CIO deploys IT resources to support critical business activities [30, 54]. However, due to the lack of qualitative studies in the IS literature, we know little about the effect of communication content on the CIO/CEO shared understanding about the role of IT.

CIO/CEO Communication Style. Communication style refers to the terms and jargon that are used by an organization's CIO and CEO to communicate about IT themes [14]. CIOs can proactively create a shared understanding of the technological side with the CEO by focusing on communicating in business terms and avoiding technical jargon that others who are not familiar with IT do not understand [53, 68]. Hence, CIOs must plan the logic of their arguments in order to

---

[1]Note that face-to-face communication is 100% natural because it has been the main mode of communication throughout almost the entire period of human evolution, and therefore, as Kock [37, 38] argues, abilities in face-to-face interactions (e.g., ability to understand other people's emotions, intentions, and reasoning processes) must be part of the genetic makeup of humans. The degree of naturalness of a communication medium can be evaluated based on the degree to which it incorporates the characteristics of face-to-face interaction. The main criteria for assessing the level of naturalness include (1) two communicating people share the same context, and they are able to see and hear each other, (2) individuals can exchange communicative stimuli in real time, (3) the situation provides the ability to both convey and observe facial expressions, (4) to convey and observe body language, and (5) to convey and listen to speech. Differences in media richness theory and media naturalness theory are discussed in Kock [37, 38].

communicate complex technical matters appropriately, and must be capable of making tacit IT knowledge explicit [9, 50]. Clarity of the explanations of potential benefits and uses of IT increases CEOs' technical knowledge, thereby also increasing motivation to communicate back with the CIO [4]. CEOs who explain organizational strategies, processes, and needs in a manner that CIOs with a technical background can understand are more effective in creating a shared understanding of the business side [35].

CIO/CEO Personal Characteristics. CIO/CEO personal characteristics (i.e., their technical and business knowledge, their working style, and their attitude toward IT) are critical for the success of championing IT within organizations. When CIOs possess knowledge about the organization's goals, objectives, and visions, they are better able to decide how IT should support and/or enable the business [31, 40]. When CEOs understand the capabilities and contribution of IT to business, they are better able to decide how IT can be employed to support the business strategy and value-chain activities [42, 70]. Hence, CIOs' educational efforts in transferring IT knowledge to the CEO are important in promoting a shared CIO/CEO understanding of the role of IT in an organization [4, 52]. A CEO's positive attitude toward IT and a CEO's willingness to discuss IT themes with the CIO contributes to the development of a shared IT understanding [34]. However, today it is not clear how the CIO/CEO personal characteristics are related to the nature of CIO/CEO communication.

Effectivity of CIO/CEO Communication. Communication is defined as a cyclical process that involves the exchange of information between individuals in order to reach a common perception and/or collective action [22, 62]. Based on this definition, we argue that effective CIO/CEO communication requires regular exchange of relevant information between the two executives, which, in turn, leads to higher levels of shared CIO/CEO understanding about the role of IT in the organization. Based on our discussion of related work, we further argue that using appropriate communication styles and a natural communication channel is critical for communication effectiveness. Moreover, we stress that empirical evidence about the link between communication effectivity and shared IT understanding hardly exists. Yet, there is reason to assume that higher communication effectivity may lead to higher shared IT understanding.

Shared CIO/CEO Understanding of the Role of IT. Shared understanding is defined as the degree of convergence between the views of an organization's CIO and CEO about the role of IT within the business [27, 62]. A shared understanding exists when the CEO understands IT objectives and the CIO understands business objectives, and both executives agree on how IT should be deployed to support or enable the business strategy. Research indicates that if such a shared understanding between the CIO and CEO about the role of IT exists, then both executives are more likely to contribute to desired organizational outcomes, such as IT strategic alignment and higher firm performance [5, 35]. Also, it was found that a shared understanding positively relates to the performance of the IT function, as well as to the success of the CIO [31, 47].

Next, we describe the research methodology that we used to gain better insight into the nature of CIO/CEO communication effectivity.

3 Research Methodology

3.1 Sampling Strategy

It is a well-known fact in the research community that it is difficult to convince top managers to serve as informants, particularly to participate in a time-consuming qualitative interview. To gain access to CEOs and CIOs (or the highest ranking IT executive within a company), we had to rely on the personal contacts of a well-connected former CIO of a multinational company located in Austria who had expressed support for our research project. As a first step, our supporter set up an initial list of forty CIOs from medium to large companies across different industries located in Austria where he has direct access to many CIOs. We discussed this list together and decided to contact all CIOs via e-mail and telephone in order to explain the research project and our domain of interest. Out of forty CIOs, twelve CIOs agreed to participate. All of these twelve CIOs agreed to talk to their respective CEOs about the study, and all twelve CEOs also agreed to serve as informants. Thus, the final sample in the present study consists of 24 top managers (12 CIOs and 12 CEOs) of twelve companies. Table 2 shows major characteristics of the participating firms.

Table 2 Organizational characteristics of the sample

Comp. ID	Industry	Number of employees[a]	Revenue in € millions[a]	Top management consists of[a]
A	Manufacturing	1500	800	CEO, CFO, CTO
B	Manufacturing	800	250	CEO, CTO
C	Manufacturing	500	150	CEO, CFO
D	Retail Trade	2500	1000	CEO, CFO, 4 × head of division
E	Retail Trade	3500	500	CEO, COO, CMO
F	Manufacturing	200	20	CEO
G	Manufacturing	6500	2000	CEO, CFO, COO, CCO
H	Manufacturing	400	80	CEO
I	Manufacturing	6000	1000	CEO, CFO, COO, CMO
J	Manufacturing	2500	800	CEO, CFO, CTO
K	Manufacturing	1500	250	CEO
L	Manufacturing	7500	1000	CEO, COO, CMO

Notes [a]Data collected from the annual reports. *CCO* Chief commercial officer, *CEO* Chief executive officer, *CMO* Chief marketing and sales officer, *COO* Chief operating officer, *CTO* chief technology officer. In order to guarantee anonymity, classification of industry is based on the highest possible abstraction level; also, we rounded the number of employees and revenues

3.2   Interview Design

Based on our research model in Fig. 1, we designed an initial set of two interview guides: one for the CIO and one for the CEO. These guides are organized around four interview sections [7] to gain insights about a wide range of factors related to CIO/CEO communication that are currently not addressed in IS research.

The first section contains a set of general questions concerning the participating person and the company. All participants are asked questions about their career background and how they would define the term "information technology" within their company. The CIO guide contains some additional questions about the CIO working environment to better understand the CIO hierarchical position and structural power. The second section uses free associations in order to capture the participants' unstructured representations of CIO/CEO communication and the IT within their company. By way of free association, participants are told a topic on which they should name the first five terms that come spontaneously into their minds [48]. Research suggests that free associations provide an insight into individual knowledge structures and are therefore well-suited to investigating mental representations empirically [23, 48]. The third section contains a typical interview section consisting of a series of open-ended questions, plus some Likert-type scales. Following previous studies (e.g., [17]), we used seven-point Likert-type scales to grade the effectiveness of the CIO/CEO communication and the CIO/CEO perception of IT importance for the business. The fourth and final section summarizes the discussion and provides an opportunity for each participant to add further comments.

The content validity of the interview guides was examined prior to the interviews. A senior consultant from a multinational technology and consulting company with longstanding experience in our research area was asked to initially review each interview guide. His valuable comments and suggestions were used to revise the initial guides. The revised guides were then piloted with an additional CIO/CEO pair from an international company (not part of the sample in the main study). The first and second author of this book met with the executives of this company for the interview. During the interviews, the authors took extensive notes on the entire interview process in order to enhance the accuracy of the data collection instrument. After completion of the interviews, each executive provided further feedback and comments about the instrument. This pre-test resulted in a second revision and adjustment of the interview guides. The final interview guides are available in Appendix A.

3.3   Data Collection

The entire data collection process covered the first half of the year 2014. During an initial orientation phase, participants were given the opportunity to ask questions regarding the study's purpose and were promised confidentiality. A confidentiality agreement was signed by the interviewer and the interviewee assuring that the data will only be used anonymously for research purposes. All interviews were conducted in the German language and tape recorded by the second author of this book (all interviews took place in Austria). The interviewer worked to elicit an interviewee's own views and ideas in order to better understand the nature, antecedents, and effects of CIO/CEO communication. Rather than directing questions toward identification of the critical communication attributes, the interviewer asked open-ended questions to give each interviewee the opportunity to speak in his or her own voice, as well as to guide the discussion into particular directions of interest. Due to this interview style, the interviews lasted up to 60 min and provided thick data in our domain of interest. Table 3 shows the profiles of all participating top managers.

3.4   Data Analysis

Before starting the data analysis procedure, we transcribed all tape recorded interviews of the 24 top managers and simplified their accentuation in order to standardize the data and to facilitate qualitative content analyses [7]. The tape recorded interviews with a total duration of more than 13 h resulted in transcripts with a total length of 206 pages of text (the CIO transcripts have a length of 108 pages of text, the CEO transcripts have a length of 98 pages of text). More detailed information about each interview is available in Appendix B.

The first step in our data analysis was to categorize (i) the level of CIO/CEO communication effectivity and (ii) the level of shared CIO/CEO understanding of the role of IT (see Appendix C for a detailed explanation of the categorization process). Then, we analyzed the interview data in order to identify text passages that include information about the nature of CIO/CEO communication. To mitigate potential bias due to coding and structuring of the transcripts, the first author of this book, who had not taken part in the interviews, performed the initial analysis. Thereby, the first author read all transcripts and marked and coded the relevant phrases by using qualitative data analysis software (ATLAS.ti) in order to make the analysis process transparent. After coding by the first author, the other two authors reviewed the results. The two main goals of this review process were the identification of inappropriate coding and the extraction of additional text passages that contain useful information about our research domain. At the end of this review process, we discussed all coding results together, and after some minor modifications and clarifications, we agreed on the final coding tables.

Table 3 Profile of the participating top managers

	CIO absolute frequency	CEO absolute frequency	CIO relative frequency (%)	CEO relative frequency (%)
Educational level				
Doctorate	1	3	8.3	25.0
Diploma and master	8	6	66.7	50.0
Bachelor	0	0	0.0	0.0
Lower educational level	3	3	25.0	25.0
Educational field				
Computer science	2	1	16.7	8.3
Economic sciences	3	6	25.0	50.0
Engineering sciences	2	2	16.7	16.7
Information systems	4	1	33.3	8.3
Law	0	2	0.0	16.7
Mathematics	1	0	8.3	0.0
Years of employment in current organization				
13 or more	3	2	25.0	16.7
10–12	1	1	8.3	8.3
7–9	4	1	33.3	8.3
4–6	3	5	25.0	41.7
3 or fewer	1	3	8.3	25.0
Former field of work				
Business	1	7	8.3	58.3
IT	10	3	83.4	25.0
Technical	1	2	8.3	16.7
Type of recruitment				
Internal hire	5	8	41.7	66.7
External hire	7	4	58.3	33.3
Gender				
Male	12	12	100.0	100.0
Female	0	0	0.0	0.0

4   Results

4.1   CIO Hierarchical Position

Table 4 shows that nine out of twelve CIOs in our sample operate at the second management level, while the three remaining CIOs operate in a staff function or external function within the company. Nonetheless, all CIOs in our sample have direct access to the top management due to their reporting line, which means that the CIO reports directly to the CEO, the CFO (chief financial officer), the COO

Table 4 CIO hierarchical position

Comp. ID	CIO management level or operating function	CIO reporting line to	CIO has regular meetings with	CIO participation in top management meetings	CIO participation in the strategic IT planning	CIO responsibility for other functions
A	2nd management level	CFO	CFO and CEO	No	Yes (IT steering committee)	No
B	Staff function	CEO	CEO	No	No	Organizational development
C	2nd management level	CEO	CEO and CFO	No	No	No
D	Staff function	CFO	CFO and CEO	Yes (informally)	Yes (management meetings)	No
E	2nd management level	CEO	CEO	No	No	Organizational development
F	2nd management level	CEO	CEO	No	No	Financial controlling
G	2nd management level	CFO	CFO and CEO	No	No	No
H	2nd management level	CEO	CEO	No	No	No
I	2nd management level	COO	COO	Yes (informally)	Yes (management meetings)	No
J	2nd management level	CFO and CTO	CFO and CTO	Yes (informally)	Yes (IT steering committee)	No
K	External function	CEO	CEO	No	No	No
L	2nd management level	CEO	CEO	No	No	No

(chief operating officer), or the CTO (chief technology officer). Through this top management access, almost all CIOs have regular meetings with their CEOs (and other top managers). Those CIOs who have no regular meetings with their CEOs participate informally in their companies' top management meetings, and therefore also have access to the CEO. Regarding CIO responsibility for other organizational functions, Table 4 shows that most CIOs are responsible exclusively for the IT function (in 75% of the cases); only in a few cases does the CIO have to assume responsibility for other functions such as organizational development or financial controlling. Thus, most CIOs in our sample can focus on their IT function and do not have to think about other responsibilities.

Despite the high hierarchical position of the CIOs in our sample, it is surprising that only four out of twelve CIOs are involved in the strategic planning of IT. A closer look reveals that those four CIOs who are involved in the strategic IT planning do not report to the CEO (they report to the CFO, COO, or CTO), but they are in general informal participants in their companies' top management meetings. The CIO of Company A is not a member of the top management, but he has a seat on the IT steering committee together with the CEO and other business unit managers, and is therefore involved in strategic IT decisions. Attendance at strategic IT meetings is critical for CIOs in order to be able to align IT with the business processes and business strategy [10, 40] and also to initiate IT projects that leverage the contribution of IT to business performance [11, 56]. In those companies where the CIO is not involved in strategic IT decisions, the CIO has hardly any access to information that is necessary to carry out the responsibilities. The CIO of Company B with twenty company sites in fourteen European countries, and the CIO of Company D, clearly expressed the significance of CIO attendance at strategic IT meetings:

> I am not invited to management meetings. This is a big disadvantage for me and also for the firm, because IT-relevant decisions are also made there, but ones where the IT is not considered. When meetings are held in the areas of organizational or corporate development in which I am not participating, it may happen that I am not informed about an initiative. Given that, it is often the case that a decision is made that is not feasible. (CIO, Company B)

> I am not a member of the top management board, but I have the opportunity to participate in management meetings in which important IT decisions are made. Therefore, it is not necessarily a disadvantage for me [if I do not always participate in top management board meetings, added by the authors of this book]. However, from the perspective of organizational influence, I think it is very important that the IT is located at the top of the company. (CIO, Company D)

IS literature often argues that a CIO should directly report to the CEO in order to promote the importance of IT and to strengthen the CIO's influence within the organization (e.g., [1, 54]). Reporting to the CFO, in contrast to reporting to the CEO, is typically considered as a diminished role of a CIO because the CIO-CFO reporting structure is often selected as a means of monitoring IT spending [3]. By contrasting the CIO-CEO reporting structure (seven CIOs in our sample report to the CEO) with the CIO-CFO reporting structure (four CIOs in our sample report to the CFO), we found that all CIOs who report to the CFO do not consider their

reporting line as an obstacle. Rather, these CIOs argue that the personal characteristics of the top manager to whom they report are the key criterion for successful
interaction (e.g., it makes a difference if a top manager has a positive attitude
toward IT or not). We asked CIOs who report to the CFO if they saw any disad-
vantages in their reporting line, and they provided comments as the following ones:

> No, not in the current situation, because from a personality perspective the CFO is much
> more IT-savvy than the CEO. The CFO is 42 years old and has a totally different view on
> IT. The CEO, however, is 64 years old and held his first smart phone in his hand recently.
> (CIO, Company A)

> Yes and no. Yes, because I am basically convinced that IT plays a key role in the orga-
> nization, and hence the CIO should directly report to the CEO. No, because in our case the
> CFO, just like the CEO, has a perspective that encompasses the entire organization ... and
> therefore it is ok for me. (CIO, Company D)

> It depends on the CFO type. A CFO who is able to realize that IT can make a valuable
> contribution and that IT is an important factor ... then this CFO will be last person who
> prevents an investment [in IT]. (CIO, Company G)

4.2 CIO/CEO Communication Frequency

Prior quantitative empirical studies (listed in Table 1) indicate that CIOs should
communicate as often as possible with their CEOs in order to reach a high level of
shared understanding on the role of IT. In contrast to this research stream, however,
our interview data reveals that almost all CIO/CEO pairs in our sample with a high
level of communication effectivity and a high level of shared understanding
regarding the organization's role of IT have only one, or at most, two regular
meetings per month (see Table 5). Many IT tasks (e.g., implementation of a new
operating system) typically take several weeks or month, and sometimes even years
(e.g., implementation of an ERP system), and it is therefore usually not necessary to
have meetings on a weekly basis, as clearly exemplified by the following statements:

> I do not see a need to communicate weekly with the CIO because an IT task often takes
> several weeks or months. Therefore, I am satisfied with the 14-day intervals [for our regular
> meetings]. (CEO, Company B)

> One meeting per month with the CIO is appropriate in my opinion. In the meetings with the
> CIO, we define general parameters and goals, so I think this is okay. (CEO, Company C)

Only two CIOs in our sample plead for regular meetings with their CEOs on a
weekly basis, because their cross-national IT projects often require quick decisions.
One of these CIOs (of Company E) communicates on a weekly basis with his CEO,
and due to this frequency, the CIO is able to align his perceptions on the ongoing IT
challenges with his CEO. As a result, they maintain a high level of shared
understanding of the role of IT. The other CIO (of Company G) who has only
monthly meetings with his CEO argues that the frequency of their regular meetings
should be increased to four times per month (i.e., to one meeting per week) in order

Table 5 CIO/CEO communication frequency

Comp. ID	Frequency of regular CIO/CEO meetings	Is this CIO/CEO meeting frequency sufficient?	Frequency of regular CIO/CFO meetings	Frequency of regular CIO/COO meetings	Frequency of CIO/CEO project-related meetings	Effectivity of CIO/CEO communication	Shared CIO/CEO understanding of the role of IT
A	1 × per month	Yes (both)	1 × per month		4 × per month	High	High
B	2 × per month	Yes (both)			Depends on project	Medium–high	High
C	1 × per month	Yes (both)	1 × per month		Depends on project	Medium	Low–medium
D	2 × per month	Yes (both)	3 × per month		Depends on project	Medium–high	Medium
E	4 × per month	Yes (both)			8 × per month	High	High
F	1 × per month	Yes (both)			1 × per month	High	Medium–high
G	1 × per month	CIO: no, CEO: yes	4 × per month		1 × per month	Medium–high	Medium–high
H	1 × every 2nd month	CIO: no, CEO: yes			Depends on project	Low	Medium
I	Not regular	Yes (both)		1 × per month	4 × per month	Medium–high	Medium–high
J	Not regular	Yes (both)	1 × per month		Depends on project	Medium–high	Medium–high
K	2 × per month	Yes (both)			Depends on project	Medium–high	Medium–high
L	1 × per month	Yes (both)			3 × per month	High	High

to further elevate their level of shared IT understanding (currently they maintain a medium to high level of shared understanding of the role of IT). With only one regular meeting per month, it is difficult for them to create common knowledge about their IT processes, and therefore to achieve effective communication.

However, ten out of twelve CIOs in our sample are satisfied with the frequency of their regular meetings with the CEOs (even when the CIO has no formal regular meetings with his CEO), as expressed in the following statements:

> The communication frequency is currently appropriate. If I need more meetings, then I can have them at any time. (CEO, Company L)

> The communication frequency [with the CEO] is appropriate. The CEO is accessible at any time for me to talk about important issues. (CIO, Company J)

The CIO of Company H is not satisfied with the frequency of regular meetings with his CEO (they only communicate every second month about IT themes). However, this CIO is faced with a completely different problem because his CEO is not interested in IT, and therefore is not willing to discuss IT issues more frequently. This CIO provided the following statement:

> Electronic data processing probably does not have the same value in the eyes of the CEO as other business areas. The priorities are elsewhere. (CIO, Company H)

With such a personal attitude of the CEO toward IT, it is difficult for the CIO to achieve effective communication with his CEO. This fact is relatively independent from the frequency of interactions. As a result, this CIO/CEO pair maintains only a medium level of communication effectivity. Also, they only have a low level of shared IT understanding.

However, with respect to CIO/CEO project-related communication, the appropriate frequency is difficult to quantify, because it depends on the requirements and complexity of the project. The following statements provide the empirical evidence for this conclusion:

> The appropriate frequency depends on the project conditions. If it is a large and critical project, you have to communicate more frequently. If it is a smaller and regular project, you communicate less. (CIO, Company A)

> From the moment when the goal of the project is clear, the communication [frequency] decreases because only the essential points are then discussed in a summarized form and the discrepancies are adjusted. (CIO, Company E)

4.3 CIO/CEO Communication Channel Naturalness

Based on our research model, we expect that CIOs and CEOs who use natural channels to communicate about IT issues with each other are more likely to achieve a high degree of shared understanding about their company's role of IT. Table 6 shows that, in total, 64% of the overall CIO/CEO communication occurs face-to-face. CIOs and CEOs stated frequently that the effectivity of their

Table 6 CIO/CEO communication channel naturalness

Comp. ID	Face-to-face	Video conference	Telephone	E-Mail	Face-to-face in %	Video conference in %	Telephone in %	E-Mail in %	Effectivity of CIO/CEO communication	Shared CIO/CEO understanding of the role of IT
A	x		x	x	60		25	15	High	High
B	x		x	x	50		5	45	Medium-high	High
C	x			x	70			30	Medium	Low-medium
D	x		x	x	50		25	25	Medium-high	Medium
E	x			x	50			50	High	High
F	x			x	85			15	High	Medium-high
G	x			x	45			55	Medium-high	Medium-high
H	x			x	55			45	Low	Medium
I	x	x	x	x	40	5	45	10	Medium-high	Medium-high
J	x				100				Medium-high	Medium-high
K	x		x	x	75		10	15	Medium-high	Medium-high
L	x	x	x	x	85	5	5	5	High	High
Sum	12	2	6	11						

communication is higher when they have face-to-face contact because this setting provides the opportunity for direct feedback and enables more comprehensive explanation of complex technical and business matters. The following quotes express the significance of face-to-face communication:

> I think the effectiveness of the communication with the CIO is influenced by the time you invest [in the meetings] and the fact that the communication process is focused [on specific topics]. Face-to-face is more effective in most situations. (CEO, Company J)

> Face-to-face contact should not be underestimated. With all the modern forms of communication that exist, I think it is critical that you still invest time [in face-to-face meetings], even if it is little. (CIO, Company B)

> Face-to-face is the foundation. I think it is important that you meet your CIO each week at least once or twice and discuss topics face-to-face. (CEO, Company L)

The CIO of Company G noted that if, for example, an alignment gap between IT and business objectives occurs, he asks his CEO for a face-to-face meeting in order to directly discuss possible solutions to reestablish strategic alignment. The CIO of Company L commented that effective communication about strategic themes (e.g., how to implement process innovations in the value chain or how to leverage existing IT assets) requires in most cases face-to-face interactions:

> If I communicated only by e-mail with the CEO, then it would be difficult, if compared to sitting together with the CIO [to discuss strategic IT themes]. Currently, our communication is good. The relationship with the CEO is very open and I am satisfied. (CIO, Company L)

The telephone is used as a communication channel by our interviewees to exchange urgent information that must be explained or commented by both parties (e.g., a resource shortage emerged during an IT project and both executives have to decide quickly how to deal with this issue). Table 6 shows that 9% of overall executive communication takes place by telephone. E-mail is the basic channel to transmit information that requires no immediate feedback from the receiver (e.g., information about the current project status, description of new IT suppliers, or IT infrastructure key performance indicators). In total, 26% of the overall executive communication is based on e-mail.

Using videoconferences for discussing IT issues is not very common in our sample, predominantly because most CIO/CEO pairs have a short distance between their offices; only 1% of the overall communication is based on videoconference. For example, the CIO of Company E is located next door to the CEO, and hence videoconferences are not necessary. However, our interviewees' noted that videoconferences could be a useful tool to exchange content rich information if one of the communication partners is located on a different company site.

4.4   CIO/CEO Communication Content

To gain insights into what topics CIOs and CEOs communicate about during their meetings, we reviewed the interview responses to determine the content of communication. Table 7 shows that the two most frequently discussed IT themes by the CIO/CEO pairs in our sample are the alignment between a company's IT and business objectives and the budget and costs of IT (ten out of twelve pairs communicate about these themes). The current and future IT projects and the company's IT strategy are the next most important topics (eight pairs communicate about it).

Table 7 indicates that in order to achieve a high level of shared understanding regarding the role of IT in a company, it is necessary that both the CIO and CEO communicate extensively about strategic topics. In fact, only those CIO/CEO pairs who discussed five or more strategic themes with each other reached a high level of shared CIO/CEO understanding of the role of IT. For example, the CEO and CIO of Company E with 3500 employees in several countries (where IT is a driver of innovation) communicate about all strategic themes listed in Table 7, and thereby are better able to develop a comprehensive understanding of the role of their IT. The CEO of this company tellingly described why he perceives strategic discussions as important and also stated reasons for this importance:

> We [the CEO and CIO] always think about the 'big picture', always based on a specific objective, and we do not discuss technological details … IT alone cannot drive business areas and strategies forward, only a very high degree of interaction with the top management and the individual business units enables us to find optimal ways to drive the firm forward in the use of IT and to be able to promote the necessary changes. This is only possible through involvement of the different organizational departments. (CEO, Company E)

When CEOs realize that strategic input from the business side is important for their CIOs to deploy IT resources to support key competitive objectives, then an important cornerstone for the development of a shared CIO/CEO understanding is laid. For example, the CIO and the CEO of Company J reached a relatively high level of shared understanding regarding the role of IT (i.e., medium-high) even though the CIO negotiates operational IT issues mainly with the CFO and the CTO (the CIO reports to both the CFO and CTO). A reason for this observation is that his CEO is aware of the importance of making strategic IT decisions directly with the CIO in order to establish an IT department that fully meets the competitive requirements, as clearly exemplified in the following statement:

> Strategic orientation is actually the only topic that I discuss with the CIO. We have split the responsibility between the CFO and CTO; they take care of the daily IT business … First and foremost, the strategic discussions provide input from me so that the CIO can do his job, for example, by explaining how the organizational structure will develop. The CIO can then decide how he wants to develop the IT function, and also how to align it [with the business]. (CEO, Company J)

CIOs have to realize that strategic input on technical matters is important for their CEOs so that they can decide appropriately how IT can enable business processes. As such, the CIO of Company I with more than 6000 employees worldwide and a revenue of 1000 million euros negotiates operational IT issues mainly with the COO (to whom the CIO reports), but he always tries to make strategic IT decisions directly with the CEO. However, strategic and operational IT issues are often interrelated, and hence the challenge is to find an appropriate

Table 7 CIO/CEO themes with respect to IT communication

Comp. ID	Business strategy	IT strategy	IT-business alignment	Competitive advantage through IT	IT innovation	IT projects	Budget and costs	IT security	Sum of IT themes	Effectivity of CIO/CEO communication	Shared CIO/CEO understanding of the role of IT
A		x	x			x	x	x	5	High	High
B	x	x	x			x	x		5	Medium–high	High
C						x	x	x	3	Medium	Low–medium
D	x	x	x	x		x	x		6	Medium–high	Medium
E	x	x	x	x	x	x	x	x	8	High	High
F			x						1	High	Medium–high
G		x	x	x		x	x	x	6	Medium–high	Medium–high
H							x		1	Low	Medium
I	x	x	x	x	x	x	x		7	Medium–high	Medium–high
J	x	x	x	x					4	Medium–high	Medium–high
K			x			x	x		3	Medium–high	Medium–high
L		x	x		x	x	x	x	5	High	High
Sum	5	8	10	5	2	9	10	5	54		

trade-off between these issues because otherwise a CEO's interest in IT topics is likely to decrease, as clearly expressed in the following statement:

> Regarding the subject of strategy definition, we [the CEO and I] have a very good understanding and communication basis. The more technical a subject is, the less understanding and interest on the subject exists. It depends entirely on the subject matter on which the communication is taking place. If it is a topic that has to do with a possible acquisition, then the interest is very high. If it is an issue that affects internal processes, the interest is rather limited ... (CIO, Company I)

Those CEOs in our sample who communicate most extensively about IT themes with their peer acted as CIO before they became CEO (the CEO of Company E communicates about eight IT themes with his CIO, and the CEO of Company I communicates about seven IT themes with his CIO). Based on this professional background, these two CEOs tend to discuss more IT-related themes with their current CIOs (compared to the other executive pairs in our sample) because they possess an extensive understanding of their companies' IT challenges.

In contrast, the CEO of Company C has a master degree in computer science, and thus he often takes over IT agendas from his CIO (e.g., the CEO is also responsible for IT-business alignment or IT innovations). Due to this CEO intervention in IT activities; problems concerning responsibility arise for the CIO because his CEO does not involve him in strategic IT decisions. In that case, it is difficult for them to perform an effective communication about strategic IT issues (their communication effectivity is only on a medium level), and consequently it is difficult for them to achieve a shared understanding about the role of IT in their company.

4.5 CIO/CEO Communication Style

Table 8 shows for each CIO (1) if he focuses on key IT issues in the communication process, (2) if he explains IT issues clearly, and (3) if he explains the IT contribution to organizational performance clearly. Moreover, Table 8 shows for each CEO (1) if he explains business needs clearly, (2) if he explains IT needs clearly, and (3) if he explains strategic IT decisions to his CIO. We reviewed the CIO responses to gain insights into the CEO communication style, and vice versa, we analyzed the CEO responses to understand the CIO communication style. As already indicated, our assumption is that this approach yields more reliable results (due to a lowered risk of the emergence of biases such as social desirability) than directly asking a person about his own behavior and performance.

Analysis of our interview data reveals that both CIOs and CEOs use, in several cases, an inappropriate communication style, and therefore struggle with communication about the role of IT in their company. Table 8 shows that only nine out of twelve CIOs have realized that is important to focus on key IT issues (e.g., how IT could and should support the business) instead of technical details (e.g., what the firm can do with a new server) in their interaction with the CEO. Time is, in general, a limiting factor for executive communication and hence CIOs have to

Table 8 CIO/CEO communication style

Comp. ID	CIO focuses on key IT issues	CIO explains IT issues clearly	CIO explains IT contribution clearly	CEO explains business needs clearly	CEO explains IT needs clearly	CEO explains strategic IT decisions	Effectivity of CIO/CEO communication	Shared CIO/CEO understanding of the role of IT
A	x	x	x			x	High	High
B	x	x	x	x		x	Medium-high	High
C		x			x		Medium	Low-medium
D	x	x	x			x	Medium-high	Medium
E	x	x	x	x	x	x	High	High
F		x			x		High	Medium-high
G	x	x	x			x	Medium-high	Medium-high
H		x					Low	Medium
I	x	x	x	x		x	Medium-high	Medium-high
J	x	x	x	x		x	Medium-high	Medium-high
K	x	x		x			Medium-high	Medium-high
L	x	x	x	x		x	High	High
Sum	9	12	8	6	3	8		

concentrate on topics that are directly relevant for IT-business success. Two CEOs tellingly described how they perceive the communication with their CIO, and the CIO of Company B clearly expressed the importance of focusing on key IT issues:

> I have sometimes only half an hour with the CEO, and therefore, I think it is critical that you are well prepared [for the meeting] to make a structured conversation possible and to focus on topics that are important for the other person. (CIO, Company B)

> We have very efficient communication. The CIO is a very organized person who addresses [IT] issues concisely and I do not need to ask a lot of questions for a long time to understand these things. (CEO, Company K)

> We have such a communication style that both sides know the important topics … The CIO is quite adept at explaining the necessities for the entire production operation … We have a shared language! (CEO, Company A)

IT issues and contributions are often very complex and difficult to understand for those without an IT background. Table 8 indicates that all CIOs in our sample are aware of the importance of explaining technical issues (e.g., gaps in security) to their CEOs in layman's terms. It is just as important as a clear explanation of technical issues by the CIO that CIOs communicate IT's contribution to business performance to their CEOs in a clear way. Despite this importance, only eight out of twelve CIOs make the value obtained from investments in IT explicit (see column "CIO explains IT contributions clearly" in Table 8). As a consequence, those CIOs who do not communicate IT's contributions to their CEOs have, in most cases, a lower level of shared understanding with them. Among these CIO/CEO pairs, the highest level of shared CIO/CEO understanding regarding the company's role of IT is "medium-high", while their lowest level of shared understanding is "low-medium". However, CIOs use different approaches to explain IT issues and the contribution of IT to their CEOs, as exemplified in the following statements:

> We [the IT team] orient ourselves strongly by the corporation's business strategies and areas … and hence the level of explanation in communication [with the CEO] is not high. All topics are prepared in such a way that everyone can understand what we are talking about. (CIO, Company E)

> I have always tried to explain [IT] topics to the CEO in a manager-friendly form and to make use of an open information policy. As a result, the CEO has a level of IT knowledge that roughly corresponds to the level that I have. Due to this shared IT knowledge, we have a very good communication basis. (CIO, Company B)

The CEO communication style also leaves room for improvement because only six out of twelve CEOs explain the company's business needs clearly to their CIOs (see column "CEO explains business needs clearly" in Table 8). Of course, in those cases in which the CIO has extensive business and organizational knowledge, it might not always be necessary that the CEO explains all business needs to the CIO, but explicit articulation can reduce ambiguity regarding business conditions in which a company operates. In particular, when a firm operates in a competitive environment where the business conditions are changing frequently, it could be difficult for the CIO to stay up-to-date. Such a scenario is described by the CEO of Company D in which the CIO has been employed for almost 30 years and hence has gained wide-ranging organizational and business knowledge (the CEO said: "The CIO knows the business inside out."), but to introduce IT innovation, the CIO nevertheless requires strong input from the business side of the company. The CIO of Company J with more than 2500 employees describes a similar scenario in which he implemented an IT innovation (i.e., a communication portal) more effectively because his CEO was able to articulate the business needs clearly to him:

> Introducing and implementing a communication platform was the subject about which we spoke. The CEO clearly defined his requirements. We then discussed the technological potentials and drawbacks, and the project evolved gradually ... as a result, we implemented this project in an optimal way. (CIO, Company J)

Table 8 shows that only three out of twelve CEOs explain IT needs clearly to their CIOs (see column "CEO explains IT needs clearly"). Those three CEOs who explain the IT needs to their CIOs in a clear way have either an educational or a professional background in IT. For example, the CEO of Company C has a university degree in computer science, and both the CEO of Company E and the CEO of Company F worked in the role of a CIO within their current companies in the past. Based on this educational or professional background in IT, the CEO can (1) advise the CIO about IT needs more effectively, (2) discuss complex IT issues with the CIO in a more technical language (without explaining and talking too much about basic technological relationships), and (3) is better able to decide how IT should be used within the business. Two interviewees clearly expressed the benefits of a CEO background in IT:

> I was the previous CIO and handed over all these [IT] things to the current CIO, and therefore, I have a strong affinity with IT ... We discuss the improvement of process efficiency through the use of IT, but also topics such as strategic IT orientation, that is, which processes should be supported by IT. (CEO, Company F)

> I can present complex technical issues to the CEO without spending hours explaining the technological background. The understanding of the advantages and disadvantages [of IT] is just there, and he often brings in arguments why we need it [or not]. The CEO also asks the right questions, so that we are better able to reflect on an issue again. (CIO, Company C)

As discussed, it is important for CIOs that they participate in strategic meetings where key IT decisions are made. Those CIOs who are not involved in such strategic meetings may have problems in carrying out their responsibilities because they have hardly any access to information that is critical for IT success. In those cases, CIOs are dependent on the willingness of their CEOs to communicate important IT decisions to them during regular meetings. Thus, if CEOs do not communicate strategic IT decisions to their CIOs the level of shared IT understanding is affected negatively.

4.6 CIO/CEO Personal Characteristics

For each CIO, Table 9 shows (1) his field of education, (2) his former field of work, (3) if he understands the business, (4) if he has a professional working style, and

(5) if he educates his CEO about the IT. For each CEO, Table 9 shows (1) his field of education, (2) his former field of work, (3) if he understands the IT, (4) if he has a positive attitude toward IT, and (5) if he takes time for discussing IT issues. We reviewed the CIO responses to gain insights into the CEO personal characteristics from numbers 3 to 5, and vice versa, we analyzed the CEO responses to understand the CIO personal characteristics from number 3 to 5. The rationale for this approach is that it is difficult to imagine that each individual CIO and CEO of our study would provide direct statements against his own competence and good manners. Thus, our assumption is that based on our approach data is less susceptible to biases, particularly social desirability.

Table 9 (column "CIO understands the business") indicates that all CEOs believe that their CIOs understand the company' goals, objectives, and vision (despite the fact that only three CIOs have an educational or professional background in economic sciences; the nine other CIOs have an IT or technical background). Profound business knowledge is important for CIOs to enable them to form a shared understanding with their CEOs regarding the business demands on IT. The CEO of Company L with more than 7500 employees worldwide and revenue of nearly 1000 million euros clearly expressed the importance of CIO business understanding; he comments on the CIO of the firm as follows:

> I think his strengths are more affected by his solid understanding of the business processes and his long affiliation with the company than by any technical details … (CEO, Company L)

Our data show that a long affiliation with the company may compensate for a missing educational background in management and economics. Hence, significant experience in a specific organizational environment implies that a CIO has learned about the company's business processes and competitive needs. The CIO of Company G with approximately 6500 employees and revenue of 2000 million euros has analyzed, and hence internalized, his company's business processes over many years to gain this business knowledge, as exemplified in the following statement:

> I have intensively analyzed our business processes … because it is essential for a CIO that he understands his business. The IT is only a part of the business … and when you do not understand the value chain, you cannot introduce innovation. (CIO, Company G)

In ten out of twelve cases the CEOs are satisfied with the CIO style of working. Due to this professional working style, the CIOs in our sample can effectively handle the (sometimes) small timeslots that they have in which to communicate about IT issues with their CEOs. As already mentioned, both the CIO with "low" communication effectivity (i.e., CIO from Company C) and the CIO with "medium" communication effectivity (i.e., CIO from Company H) have some deficits in their working style. These deficits manifest themselves predominantly in three ways: the CIO (1) is not always prepared well for the meetings with the CEO, (2) neglects to set up a structured agenda for the meetings with the CEO in which key IT issues are discussed, or (3) discusses IT projects with the CEO which are not (yet) clearly specified, and therefore misunderstandings are likely to emerge. The time available for personal meetings with the CEO is often short, and therefore such inadequacies

Table 9 CIO/CEO personal characteristics

Comp. ID	CIO field of education	CIO former field of work	CIO understands the business	CIO has a professional working style	CIO educates the CEO about IT	CEO field of education	CEO former field of work	CEO understands the IT	CEO has a positive attitude toward IT	CEO takes time for discussing IT issues	Effectivity of CIO/CEO communication	Shared CIO/CEO understanding of the role of IT
A	math.	IT	x	x	x	eng. sci.	Technical	x	x	x	High	High
B	inf. sys.	IT	x	x	x	econ. sci.	Business	x	x	x	Medium-high	High
C	inf. sys.	IT	x			comp. sci.	Business	x	x	x	Medium	Low-medium
D	comp. sci.	IT	x	x	x	econ. sci.	Business	x	x	x	Medium-high	Medium
E	econ. sci.	IT	x	x		econ. sci.	IT	x	x	x	High	High
F	econ. sci.	business	x	x		econ. sci.	IT	x	x	x	High	Medium-high
G	econ. sci.	IT	x	x	x	law	Business	x	x	x	Medium-high	Medium-high
H	eng. sci.	technical	x			eng. sci.	Technical				Low	Medium
I	inf. sys.	IT	x	x		inf. sys.	IT	x	x		Medium-high	Medium-high
J	comp. sci.	IT	x	x		econ. sci.	Business		x	x	Medium-high	Medium-high
K	eng. sci.	IT	x	x		econ. sci.	Business		x	x	Medium-high	Medium-high
L	inf. sys.	IT	x	x	x	Law	Business	x	x	x	High	High
Sum			12	10	5			9	11	10		

Notes comp. sci. = computer science, econ. sci. = economic sciences, eng. sci. = engineering sciences, inf. sys. = information systems, math. = mathematics make it difficult to develop a high level of a shared CIO/CEO understanding regarding the role of IT in the company. This explains why those CIOs with deficits in their working style only achieved a "low-medium" or "medium" level of shared understanding about the role of IT with their CEO (see the last column in Table 9).

The CEOs' understanding of IT is critical for CIOs to form a shared understanding regarding the capabilities and potential contributions of IT to company performance, and to be better able to decide together how IT can be employed to support the business strategy and value-chain activities. Interestingly, nine out of twelve CIOs think that their CEOs possess this required level of IT knowledge. Four of those CEOs with an appropriate level of IT understanding have an educational background in IT or have worked previously in the IT field. In the other five companies where the CEO had insufficient IT knowledge, the CIO had educated the CEO about IT in order to create/provide this IT knowledge (i.e., what IT can do and what one may expect from IT). The CEOs and CIOs tellingly described their perspectives on IT understanding:

> When the CIO is a technical expert and the CEO does not possess IT knowledge, then I think it is very difficult for the CEO to talk with the technical expert, or at least to understand what he is saying. (CEO, Company G)

> If I had not been the CIO previously, I think that communication with the CIO would be quite difficult. An advantage [of my IT background] is that I can understand and judge the things the company needs and those it does not need. (CEO, Company E)

> Due to the fact that the CEO was my predecessor and really has sound IT experience, our communication is very effective. If this had not been the case, then we would have sometimes had problems in our communication. The electronic data processing knowledge of the CEO is absolutely critical, without that knowledge it would not be always easy. (CIO, Company F)

Just as important as the IT knowledge of the CEO is that the CEO has a positive attitude toward IT, because when the CEO is willing and open to discuss IT issues with the CIO, then he is better able to specify IT projects that drive the company forward in the use of IT. A negative CEO attitude toward IT adversely affects CIO/CEO communication, and in consequence also their level of shared understanding of the role of IT. The CIO of Company H has enormous problems regarding the communication about IT issues with his CEO, and hence the development of a shared IT understanding is hampered. In essence, the CEO in this company is absolutely not interested in IT, as effectively exemplified in the following statement:

> Electronic data processing has to work, and therefore I do not care about it. We need electronic data processing as a tool, and the CIO ensures that this tool works. Electronic data processing is a utility, like a car, where I start the engine and drive off. (CEO, Company H)

However, in most cases the CIOs are satisfied with the amount of time that they have to discuss IT issues with their CEOs. Moreover, the data of our sample shows that most CIOs can contact their CEOs at any time if an urgent decision has to be made, as the following examples indicate:

When there are any problems, I can always contact the CEO, also when an urgent decision must be made. (CEO, Company E)

I always have access to the CEO when I have a problem. The former CEO did not really care much about IT; the current CEO is more competent from this point of view. (CEO, Company L)

5 Discussion

Despite its theoretical and practical significance, to the best of our knowledge, no scientific study has investigated in detail the nature of effective CIO/CEO communication. Based on personal interviews with CIO/CEO pairs from twelve companies, and the little we knew a priori from the existing literature (see Sect. 2), we made a first contribution to closing this significant research gap by developing a conceptual model of CIO/CEO communication effectivity (see Fig. 2). In the following, we elaborate on the model.

The model indicates that a high hierarchical position within the organization is important for the CIO to have access to the CEO, and to be able to discuss IT themes directly with the CEO (see ❶). When the CIO does not directly communicate with the CEO about IT themes on a regular basis, information flow is impaired (e.g., see also the studies from Kearns [33] or Ragu-Nathan et al. [55]). Our interview data indicates that a high CIO hierarchical position can either be implemented by setting the CIO reporting line directly to the CEO, or by positioning the CIO at least at the second management level or an equivalent functional position.

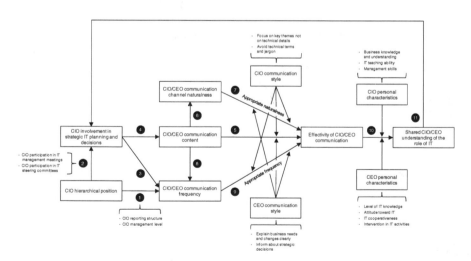

Fig. 2 Conceptual model of CIO/CEO communication

When the CIO does not operate in a high hierarchical position, then it is more likely that the CIO is not involved in management board meetings or steering committees where strategic IT planning and decisions are made (see ❷), which, in turn, adversely influences communication frequency between the CIO and CEO about IT themes (see ❸). This lack of involvement in IT planning and decisions causes problems for CIOs in carrying out their responsibilities because in that case they often have no access to information that is essential for key IT tasks (e.g., aligning IT with current and future business objectives), and have no chance to discuss, and influence, the top management's IT decisions (see ❹). A CIO exclusion from strategic IT planning may also cause problems for management teams because it could happen that top managers make an IT decision that is not feasible (e.g., replacing the old ERP system without evaluating the far-reaching consequences of such a system change).

In contrast to the extant literature (e.g., [66]), the CIOs in our sample do not, in general, see a necessity to be accepted as a formal member of the company's management board. They rather argue that involvement in IT planning and decision meetings of the management board is sufficient for them to be able to communicate with top managers about strategic IT themes effectively. One important aspect for the CIOs in our sample is, however, that they have the opportunity to discuss a wide range of IT themes with their CEOs (ranging from critical issues in IT projects to new IT innovations), and to educate and manage their CEOs' expectations on the value IT can deliver in order to achieve effective communication and a harmonized view on the role of IT (see ❺).

Our interviewees indicate that the IT themes that are discussed between the CIO and CEO influence the naturalness of their communication channel (see ❻). If the complexity of the IT themes is high (e.g., how IT should support new business processes), then the CIO/CEO pairs in our sample prefer face-to-face meetings because this channel enables a more detailed explanation of complex business and technical objectives. However, they indicate that a lower degree of naturalness is sufficient (e.g., communication via telephone or e-mail), if the IT themes do not require detailed explanation and are simple to understand (e.g., the CIO informs the CEO about implementation progress of a new IT system). Thus, with an appropriate degree of naturalness, CIOs and CEOs can achieve a higher level of communication effectivity (see ❼).

In contrast to prior studies, our results demonstrate that an appropriate communication frequency between the CIO and CEO is more suitable to achieve a high level of shared understanding regarding the company's role of IT; too many interactions may adversely affect communication effectivity. CEOs have to manage multiple organizational issues during their work time, and therefore, it is not wise for CIOs to take as much time as possible of their CEOs to discuss IT themes. Concerning the term "appropriate frequency", the CIOs and CEOs in our sample suggest that one or two regular CIO/CEO meetings per month are usually enough in most cases because strategic IT tasks (e.g., developing a new IT system for supporting the supply chain) often last several month, and sometimes even years. Our model therefore shows that the communication theme between the CIO and CEO should determine the frequency of their interactions (see ❽), and an appropriate frequency in their interactions leads, in turn, to an effective IT communication (see ❾).

Analysis of the transcripts revealed that communication style is an important determinant of communication effectivity. To gain benefits from personal meetings, both executives are encouraged to keep focused on key issues during their meetings, and to avoid jargon and other terms that either the CEO, or CIO, does not understand (see ❿). CIOs have to concentrate on topics that are directly relevant for IT-business success, and have to explain technical issues and the contribution of IT to their CEOs in a clear way. CEOs, in contrast, have to explain business needs clearly to their CIOs to reduce ambiguity concerning business processes and requirements, and have to inform their CIOs proactively about strategic decisions that may affect the IT domain. When both executives achieve shared language, then it is more likely that their communication effectivity is high. In Fig. 2, we illustrate these insights with the factor 'CIO/CEO communication style' as moderator between the CIO/CEO communication attributes (communication channel, communication content and communication frequency) and the effectivity of CIO/CEO communication.

CIO/CEO communication effectivity, in turn, influences the level of shared understanding between the CIO and CEO regarding the role of IT. As illustrated in Fig. 3, in seven out of twelve cases, the level of CIO/CEO communication effectivity and the level of shared CIO/CEO understanding of the role of IT are identical. In four cases, there is only one level difference between communication effectivity and shared understanding (e.g., CIO/CEO communication effectivity is 'high' while shared CIO/CEO understanding is 'medium-high'). Only in one out of twelve cases

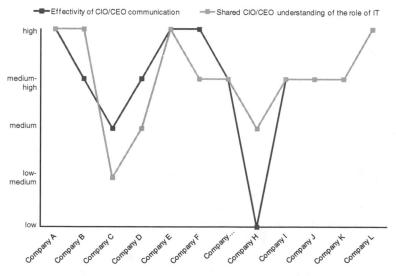

Fig. 3 CIO/CEO communication effectivity and shared CIO/CEO understanding of the role of IT

there is a difference of two levels (Company H: communication effectivity is 'low' and shared understanding is 'medium'). Despite the fact that one should not generalize qualitative data to develop a nomothetic law, our results clearly indicate a positive relationship between communication effectivity and shared understanding.

Based on the interviewees' responses, we conclude that the personal characteristics of the CIO and CEO affect their communication pattern, and consequently also their level of shared understanding. When a CEO possesses at least basic IT knowledge, has a positive attitude toward IT, and/or possesses IT cooperativeness, then the foundation for developing a shared IT understanding regarding the role of IT is laid. Recent evidence supports this reasoning by arguing that a CIO's ability to foster change is greater when the CIO communicates with someone who believes in, and understands, the importance of IT [3, 39]. When CIOs understand their business in detail, have a professional style of working (e.g., CIO/CEO meetings are prepared well), and/or are good IT educators, then this shared CIO/CEO understanding can grow. In Fig. 2, we summarize these insights with the factor 'CIO/CEO personal characteristics' which moderates all communication effects on shared CIO/CEO understanding of the role of IT.

The extent to which CEOs participate in strategic IT discussions is influenced by their IT knowledge [20]. If a CEO possesses an educational background in IT, or has worked previously in the IT domain, then the CEO will more likely take an active part in IT activities, and also propose IT initiatives by himself. Such a CEO involvement in IT activities is important for the CIO to fully leverage the potential of IT [69], but some CIOs in our sample indicate that when a CEO intervenes too much in the management of IT, then the effectivity of communication decreases and the CIO's job becomes more difficult. Thus, the appropriate level of CEO intervention in IT activities is an important aspect of the CEO personal characteristics that requires future investigation.

Finally, our interview data reveals that the degree of shared understanding between the CIO and CEO may affect the level of CIO involvement in strategic IT planning and decisions (see ❶). If the CEO and other top managers recognize the importance of discussing strategic objectives with the CIO where the IT is involved, then the CIO may be better able to implement specific IT systems to drive the company forward in the use of IT, which, in turn can leverage desired business outcomes.

To exemplify our findings in more detail, we discuss the conceptual model (Fig. 2) based on two different CIO/CEO pairs. The first CIO/CEO pair is from Company E where both executives have a 'high' level of communication effectivity and a 'high' level of shared understanding of the role of IT (a "positive" case). The second CIO/CEO pair is from Company H where both executives have, in contrast, a 'low' level of communication effectivity and a 'medium' level of shared understanding (a "negative" case). Based on the interviewees' responses and our conceptual model, we discuss their communication patterns.

The CIO of Company E operates at the second management level but reports directly to the CEO. However, he does neither participate in strategic IT planning meetings, nor is he involved in top management meetings where key IT decisions are made. The main reason for this CIO exclusion from strategic IT decisions is that the CEO of this company acted as CIO before he became the CEO, and therefore the CEO takes on responsibility for strategic IT decisions. However, this exclusion is not an issue for the CIO because the CEO informs him about all important IT and business decisions, and also discusses the resulting implications with him.

With respect to hierarchical position, the CIO of Company H also operates at the second management level and directly reports to the CEO. Moreover, this CIO is not involved in strategic IT planning and decision meetings either. However, the notable difference to Company E is that the CEO of Company H is not interested in IT, and this CEO also believes that IT has not the capability to strategically drive the organization forward. Consequently, the CIO and CEO of Company H communicate only every second month formally about IT themes. During these meetings, they only discuss budget and cost issues, but do not speak about strategic themes such as IT innovations or IT-business alignment. This communication frequency, at least in this case, does not allow for the creation of a shared IT vision. In contrast, the CIO and CEO of Company E communicate at least once a week about IT and business issues. The CEO of Company E stated that he communicates with his CIO about all topics that may contribute to their shared understanding of the role of IT. In this context, it has to be noted that both executives sit next-door, and therefore it is easy to communicate frequently.

The CIO of Company E is always well prepared for the meetings with the CEO and focuses mostly on key IT issues in the meetings. Moreover, the CIO of Company E explains IT issues and IT contributions clearly to his CEO, a fact which positively affects communication effectivity. Both executives frequently use technical terms during their meetings to discuss complex IT issues, but this does not adversely affect their communication effectivity because the CEO possesses profound technical knowledge. In Company H, however, the CEO has no technical background (and is not willing to change this situation due to his disinterest in IT), and therefore the CIO has to take care which terms and jargon he uses in his communication with the CEO. The CIO of Company H, however, has difficulties in explaining the contribution of IT to his CEO, and he is not always well-prepared for the meetings with the CEO. This also negatively affects communication effectivity.

As noted above, the CEO of Company H does not believe in the strategic potential of IT, and therefore, from his point of view, it is not necessary to provide business-related information to his CIO. However, business-related information would be important for the CIO in order to learn more about organizational processes and requirements, which, in turn, forms the basis for IT-business alignment.

6 Implications

From our interview data, we have learned that if the top management of a company does not implement an appropriate hierarchical position for the CIO (i.e., neither invites the CIO to top management meetings nor implements an appropriate CIO reporting line), then it is difficult for the CIO to communicate about IT issues with the CEO in an effective manner. Directly reporting to the CEO is not always necessary. However, what is necessary for CIOs is that they are involved in the strategic IT planning meetings and decisions, or in the IT steering committee, so that they have access to information that is critical for IT success and can ensure that only feasible IT decisions are made. If the CEO and other top managers have failed to set up an appropriate working environment for the CIO, the CIO should try to lobby the top management to invite him to meetings where important IT plans and decisions are made. If no changes occur, the CIO should accept the existing structure and work to ensure communication with the CEO and other executives who perform functions crucial for CIO success.

Both CIOs and CEOs can use our model illustrated in Fig. 2 to ensure a high level of effectiveness in their communication. First, CIOs and CEOs should recognize that the content of their communication should determine communication frequency and whether face-to-face communication is required. Complex themes should be discussed face-to-face because this setting provides the opportunity for immediate feedback, perception of facial expressions and body language, and hence leads (more quickly) to a shared understanding due to lower levels of communication ambiguity. Simple information sharing (e.g., communication on IT project status) should be based on media such as e-mail (to save CEO working time). It is important to note that most executives in our sample do not see a need to discuss IT themes on a weekly base with the CEO. Rather, in most cases less frequent face-to-face communication with the CEO is sufficient.

CIOs and CEOs benefit most from their regular meetings when they focus on key issues and avoid jargon and terms in the communication process that a layperson would not understand. This means, for example, that CIOs should focus on key IT issues (i.e., how IT supports or enables the business), and explain those IT issues in clear terms and without jargon so that others without a technical background can understand them. Of course, if the CEO has a technical background, the CIO can use technical language (in our sample the CEO of Company C has a university degree in computer science, and thus, communicates effectively with his CIO in technical language). However, if CEOs do not possess the required level of IT knowledge, CIOs should educate their CEOs about IT capabilities, and especially, manage their expectations of IT in order to achieve higher levels of communication effectivity. One of the most important issues for CIOs is to clearly demonstrate and argue the contribution made by IT products and services to business performance because awareness of this track of record can positively influence the CEO's view of and attitude toward IT.

CEOs should explain business needs clearly to their CIOs so that business and IT capabilities are integrated into powerful technical solutions. Especially if CIOs are not involved in the IT meetings of the top management, CEOs should communicate important strategic decisions that affect the overall IT function to their CIOs so that they can align the IT resources with the changing business environment, and decide together how IT can transform future business processes.

When CIOs involve their CEOs actively in strategic IT initiatives, then CEOs can learn about the capabilities of IT, and therefore, are better able to recognize how IT contributes to certain business activities. However, when CEOs intervene too much in IT activities, then problems concerning responsibility may arise for the CIO. If CEOs possess no educational or professional background in IT, CEOs should not advise their CIOs about strategic IT initiatives because they may thereby introduce unnecessary limitations of a predominantly technological nature.

7   Limitations and Future Research

We explored a wide range of ideas associated with CEO/CIO communication in order to gain insights into how these ideas fit together. Despite our comprehensive and accurate research approach, we have to note as a limitation that all companies in our sample are located in Austria. Research indicates that the national context may have an influence on the development of a shared CIO/CEO understanding regarding the role of IT [19, 54], and therefore, as a function of culture, different communication patterns may lead to shared understanding of IT. The CIOs in our sample, for example, argue that they do not see the necessity to be included in the management board as formal member to communicate effectively about IT themes with the CEO. However, it is possible that this point of view may be limited to German-speaking countries, because CIO membership in the management board is not very common in Austria, Germany, and Switzerland [25, 59]. To enhance knowledge about CIO/CEO communication effectiveness in different cultures, researchers are encouraged to use our conceptual model (Fig. 2) to replicate our study in other geographical regions.

Moreover, researchers could formally test our model in a large-scale survey, or use mixed methods research to verify the findings of our study. For example, researchers could investigate the link between an appropriate frequency of CIO/CEO communication about IT themes and their level of communication effectivity and level of shared understanding of the role of IT. Also, no related work does exist on communication content's effects on CIO/CEO communication effectivity and shared IT understanding. Our study is a first step that provides evidence for the proposition that the communication content should determine communication frequency and communication channel naturalness.

After several reviews of our interview data, a new factor appeared that should be considered in future CIO/CEO communication research, namely the CEO intervention in IT management. Future research is encouraged to quantify the appropriate level of CEO intervention in IT activities, as well as the factors that determine this appropriate level. Moreover, it is crucial to examine the potential effects of CEO intervention on outcome variables such as performance of the IT function or success of the CIO [31, 47].

Another point for model extension is that leadership behavior and decision making depends on a top manager's personality, and thus, personality (e.g., need for dominance) could influence CIO/CEO communication [18]. Some CIOs in our sample stated that CEO personality could be an important attribute in determining how a face-to-face meeting runs. Finally, communication and trust have an interaction effect in some cases. Without trust, the CEO may not communicate with the CIO about key strategic objectives, and may not trust the CIO's judgement about the capabilities and benefits of IT, which makes the CIO's educational efforts more difficult. The level of trust between a firm's CIO and CEO can be specified more precisely based on relevant literature. For example, Mayer et al. [45] describe and measure the trustworthiness of an individual with three dimensions: ability (i.e., skills and competencies that are important for a relationship), benevolence (i.e., how well-meaning the interaction partner is aside from an egocentric motive), and integrity (i.e., how well the interaction partner adheres to principles and laws that the other person finds acceptable). Researchers could use Mayer et al.'s [45] trustworthiness framework together with our communication model to measure the interaction effects between communication and trust. Whatever avenue IS scholars choose to continue the current paper's line of research, it will be rewarding to see what insights future research will reveal.

A methodological conclusion that can be drawn from Table 1 is that survey and case study have hitherto been the dominant methods in CIO/CEO communication research, and in the present paper we applied an interview approach. It is likely that future mixed methods research provides the greatest potential for further novel insights. A recent paper by Venkatesh et al. [72] outlines the enormous value of mixed methods research in the IS field in general. Specifically, the Venkatesh et al. [72] study indicates seven purposes of mixed methods research (see Table 1 in their paper, p. 26), several of which are also of relevance for CIO/CEO communication. For example, completeness (i.e. mixed methods are used in order to gain complementary views about the same phenomenon or relationships), compensation (i.e., mixed methods enable compensating for the weaknesses of one approach by using the other), and diversity (i.e., mixed methods are used with the hope of obtaining divergent views of the same phenomenon) are essential purposes for mixed methods studies, and will hopefully motivate future mixed methods studies in the CIO/CEO communication domain.

By analyzing the country in which previous CIO/CEO communication studies collected their data, it becomes evident that IS research has been predominantly performed in the United States and a few other English-speaking countries (e.g., Australia and Canada). Due to the fact that both cultural and legal aspects may affect CIO and CEO behavior (e.g., [43]), we make a call for more culturally diverse studies. Especially, in countries which have been mostly neglected in prior studies more research is needed (e.g., CIO research in Asia or in the German-speaking area is scarce).

Finally, we have to note that despite our accurate research methodology, the presented interpretation of the interview statements cannot be free from our own, sometimes even unconscious, beliefs. In this context, the Hungarian-British polymath Michael Polanyi (1891–1976) argues in his book "Personal Knowledge" that objectivity is a false ideal, because all knowledge claims rely, at least to some extent, on personal judgments [51]. Similar notions can be found in IS literature. For example, Walsham [73], citing the American anthropologist Clifford Geertz, writes: "What we call our data are really our own constructions of other people's constructions of what they and their compatriots are up to" (p. 320). The kind of research presented in this paper is deeply rooted in a hermeneutic tradition, thereby being of a fundamentally idiographic nature. Such research, therefore, has the objective of providing "richness in reality", and not "tightness of control" ([44], p. 308). If follows that the present study is a first contribution to an important research field; however, more research is needed to confirm, extend, or revise the findings of the present study.

Acknowledgments We thank all scholars and anonymous reviewers for their efforts in providing guidance on ways to improve this work.

References

1. Al-Taie, M., Lane, M., Cater-Steel, A.: The relationship between organisational strategic IT vision and CIO roles: one size does not fit all. Australas. J. Inf. Syst. **18**(2), 59–89 (2014)
2. Armstrong, C.P., Sambamurthy, V.: Information technology assimilation in firms: the influence of senior leadership and IT infrastructures. Inf. Syst. Res. **10**(4), 304–327 (1999)
3. Banker, R.D., Hu, N., Pavlou, P.A., Luftman, J.: CIO reporting structure, strategic positioning, and firm performance. MIS Q. **35**(2), 487–504 (2011)
4. Bassellier, G., Benbasat, I., Reich, B.H.: The influence of business managers' IT competence on championing IT. Inf. Syst. Res. **14**(4), 317–336 (2003)
5. Benlian, A., Haffke, I.: Does mutuality matter? Examining the bilateral nature and effects of CEO-CIO mutual understanding. J. Strateg. Inf. Syst. **25**(2), 104–126 (2016)
6. Bostrom, R.N.: Competence in Communication: A Multidisciplinary Approach. Sage Publications, Beverly Hills (2016)
7. Bryman, A., Bell, E.: Business Research Methods, 3rd edn. Oxford University Press, New York (2011)
8. Chan, Y.E., Sabherwal, R., Thatcher, J.B.: Antecedents and outcomes of strategic IS alignment: an empirical investigation. IEEE Trans. Eng. Manag. **53**(1), 27–47 (2006)
9. Chen, Y.-C., Wu, J.-H.: IT management capability and its impact on the performance of a CIO. Inf. Manag. **48**(4/5), 145–156 (2011)
10. Chen, D.Q., Preston, D.S., Xia, W.: Antecedents and effects of CIO supply-side and demand-side leadership: a staged maturity model. J. Manag. Inf. Syst. **27**(1), 231–271 (2010)
11. Cohen, J.F., Dennis, C.M.: Chief information officers: an empirical study of competence, organisational positioning and implications for performance. S. Afr. J. Econ. Manag. Sci **13**(2), 203–221 (2010)
12. Daft, R.L., Lengel, R.H.: Organizational information requirements, media richness, and structural design. Manag. Sci. **32**(5), 554–572 (1986)
13. Daft, R.L., Lengel, R.H., Trevino, L.K.: Message equivocality, media selection, and manager performance: Implications for information systems. MIS Q. **11**(3), 355–366 (1987)
14. Duran, R.L., Spitzberg, B.H.: Toward the development and validation of a measure of cognitive communication competence. Commun. Q. **43**(3), 259–275 (1995)
15. Earl, M.J., Feeny, D.F.: Is your CIO adding value? Sloan Manag. Rev. **35**(3), 11–20 (1994)
16. Enns, H.G., Huff, S.L., Higgins, C.A.: CIO lateral influence behaviors: Gaining peers' commitment to strategic information systems. MIS Q. **27**(1), 155–176 (2003)

17. Feeny, D.F., Edwards, B.R., Simpson, M.K.: Understanding the CEO/CIO relationship. MIS Q. **16**(4), 435–448 (1992)
18. Flauto, F.J.: Walking the talk: the relationship between leadership and communication competence. J. Leadersh. Organ. Stud. **6**(1–2), 86–97 (1999)
19. Ford, D.P., Connelly, C.E., Meister, D.B.: Information systems research and Hofstede's culture's consequences: an uneasy and incomplete partnership. IEEE Trans. Eng. Manag. **50**(1), 8–26 (2003)
20. Haffke, I., Benlian, A.: To understand or to be understood? A dyadic analysis of perceptual congruence and interdependence between CEOs and CIOs. In: Proceedings of the 34th International Conference on Information Systems (2013)
21. Hambrick, D.C., Mason, P.A.: Upper echelons: the organization as a reflection of its top managers. Acad. Manag. Rev. **9**(2), 193–206 (1984)
22. Hargie, O., Tourish, D.: Assessing the effectiveness of communication in organisations: the communication audit approach. Health Serv. Manag. Res. **6**(4), 276–285 (1993)
23. Hollway, W., Jefferson, T.: Doing Qualitative Research differently: A Psychosocial Approach, 2nd edn. SAGE Publications Ltd., London (2012)
24. Huang, K., Quaddus, M.: An analysis of IT expectations across different strategic context of innovation: the CEO versus the CIO. In: Proceedings of the Pacific Asia Conference on Information Systems, paper 190 (2008)
25. Hütter, A., Riedl, R.: Der Chief Information Officer (CIO) in Deutschland und den USA: Verbreitung und Unterschiede. Inf. Manag. Consult. **26**(3), 61–66 (2011)
26. Jarvenpaa, S.L., Ives, B.: Executive involvement and participation in the management of information technology. MIS Q. **15**(2), 205–227 (1991)
27. Johnson, A.M., Lederer, A.L.: The effect of communication frequency and channel richness on the convergence between chief executive and chief information officers. J. Manag. Inf. Syst. **22**(2), 227–252 (2005)
28. Johnson, A.M., Lederer, A.L.: The impact of communication between CEOs and CIOs on their shared views of the current and future role of IT. Inf. Syst. Manag. **24**(1), 85–90 (2007)
29. Johnson, A.M., Lederer, A.L.: CEO/CIO mutual understanding, strategic alignment, and the contribution of IS to the organization. Inf. Manag. **47**(3), 138–149 (2010)
30. Jones, M.C., Arnett, K.P.: Linkages between the CEO and the IS environment: an empirical assessment. Inf. Resour. Manag. J. **7**(1), 20–34 (1994)
31. Kaarst-Brown, M.L.: Understanding an organization's view of the CIO: the role of assumptions about IT. MIS Q. Executive **4**(2), 287–301 (2005)
32. Karimi, J., Gupta, Y.P., Somers, T.M.: The congruence between a firm's competitive strategy and information technology leader's rank and role. J. Manag. Inf. Syst. **13**(1), 63–88 (1996)
33. Kearns, G.S.: The effect of top management support of SISP on strategic IS management: insights from the US electric power industry. Omega **34**(3), 236–253 (2006)
34. Kearns, G.S., Lederer, A.L.: A resource-based view of strategic IT Alignment: how knowledge sharing creates competitive advantage. Decis. Sci. **34**(1), 1–29 (2003)
35. Kearns, G.S., Sabherwal, R.: Strategic alignment between business and information technology: a knowledge-based view of behaviors, outcome, and consequences. J. Manag. Inf. Syst. **23**(3), 129–162 (2006)
36. Kettinger, W.J., Zhang, C., Marchand, D.A.: CIO and business executive leadership approaches to establishing company-wide information orientation. MIS Q. Executive **10**(4), 157–174 (2011)
37. Kock, N.: The psychobiological model: Towards a new theory of computer-mediated communication based on Darwinian evolution. Organ. Sci. **15**(3), 327–348 (2004)
38. Kock, N.: Information systems theorizing based on evolutionary psychology: an interdisciplinary review and theory integration framework. MIS Q. **33**(2), 395–418 (2009)
39. Leidner, D.E., Mackay, J.M.: How incoming CIOs transition into their new jobs. MIS Q. Executive **6**(1), 17–28 (2007)
40. Li, Y., Tan, C.-H.: Matching business strategy and CIO characteristics: the impact on organizational performance. J. Bus. Res. **66**(2), 248–259 (2013)

41. Lind, M.R., Zmud, R.W.: The influence of a convergence in understanding between technology providers and users on technology innovativeness. Organ. Sci. **2**(2), 195–217 (1991)
42. Luftman, J., Kempaiah, R.: An update on business-IT alignment: "A line" has been drawn. MIS Q. Executive **6**(3), 165–177 (2007)
43. MacIntyre, P.D., Babin, P.A., Clement, R.: Willingness to communicate: antecedents and consequences. Commun. Q. **47**(2), 215–229 (1999)
44. Mason, R.O., KcKenney, J.L., Copeland, D.G.: An historical method for MIS research: steps and assumptions. MIS Q. **21**(3), 307–320 (1997)
45. Mayer, R.C., Davis, J.H., Schoorman, F.D.: An integrative model of organizational trust. Acad. Manag. Rev. **20**(3), 709–734 (1995)
46. McCroskey, J.C.: Communication competence and performance: a pedagogical perspective. Commun. Educ. **31**(1), 1–7 (1982)
47. Nelson, K.M., Cooprider, J.G.: The contribution of shared knowledge to IS group performance. MIS Q. **20**(4), 409–432 (1996)
48. Nelson, D.L., McEvoy, C.L., Dennis, S.: What is free association and what does it measure? Mem Cogn. **28**(6), 887–899 (2000)
49. Peppard, J.: Unlocking the performance of the chief information officer (CIO). Calif. Manag. Rev. **52**(4), 73–99 (2010)
50. Peppard, J., Edwards, C., Lambert, R.: Clarifying the ambiguous role of the CIO. MIS Q. Executive **10**(1), 31–44 (2011)
51. Polanyi, M.: Personal Knowledge: Towards a Post-critical Philosophy. University of Chicago Press, Chicago (1958)
52. Preston, D.S., Karahanna, E.: Mechanisms for the development of shared mental models between the CIO and the top management team In: Proceedings of the 25th International Conference on Information Systems, paper 37 (2004)
53. Preston, D.S., Karahanna, E.: How to develop a shared vision: the key to IS strategic alignment. MIS Q. Executive **8**(1), 1–8 (2009)
54. Preston, D.S., Karahanna, E., Rowe, F.: Development of shared understanding between the chief information officer and top management team in U.S. and French organizations: a cross-cultural comparison. IEEE Trans. Eng. Manag. **53**(2), 191–206 (2006)
55. Ragu-Nathan, B.S., Apigian, C.H., Ragu-Nathan, T.S., Tu, Q.: A path analytic study of the effect of top management support for information systems performance. Omega **32**(6), 459–471 (2004)
56. Ranganathan, C, Jha, S.: Do CIOs matter? Assessing the value of CIO presence in top management teams. In: Proceedings of the 29th International Conference on Information Systems, paper 56 (2008)
57. Rattanasampan, W., Chaidaroon, S.: The applications of communication competence framework for CIOs. In: Proceedings of the 9th Americas Conference on Information Systems, paper 160 (2003)
58. Reich, B.H., Benbasat, I.: Factors that influence the social dimension of alignment between business and information technology objectives. MIS Q. **24**(1), 81–113 (2000)
59. Riedl, R., Kobler, M., Roithmayr, F.: Zur personellen Verankerung der IT-Funktion im Vorstand börsennotierter Unternehmen: Ergebnisse einer inhaltsanalytischen Betrachtung. Wirtschaftsinformatik **50**(2), 111–128 (2008)
60. Riedl, R., Rückel, D.: Historical development of research methods in the information systems discipline. In: Proceedings of the 17th Americas Conference on Information Systems, paper 28 (2011)
61. Rockart, J.F., Earl, M.J., Ross, J.W.: Eight imperatives for the new IT organization. Sloan Manag. Rev. **38**(1), 43–55 (1996)
62. Rogers, E.M., Kincaid, D.L.: Communication Networks: Toward a New Paradigm for Research. Free Press, New York (1981)
63. Ross, J.W., Beath, C.M., Goodhue, D.L.: Develop long-term competitiveness through IT assets. Sloan Manag. Rev. **38**(1), 31–42 (1996)

64. Rubin, R.B., Martin, M.M., Bruning, S.S., Powers, D.E.: Test of self-efficacy model of interpersonal communication competence. Commun. Q. **47**(2), 210–220 (1993)
65. Sarker, S., Xiao, X., Beaulieu, T.: Qualitative studies in information systems: a critical review and some guiding principles. MIS Q. **37**(4), iii–xviii (2013)
66. Smaltz, D.H., Sambamurthy, V., Agarwal, R.: The antecedents of CIO role effectiveness in organizations: an empirical study in the healthcare sector. IEEE Trans. Eng. Manag. **53**(2), 207–222 (2006)
67. Spitze, J.M., Lee, J.J.: The renaissance CIO project: the invisible factors of extraordinary success. Calif. Manag. Rev. **54**(2), 72–91 (2012)
68. Stephens, C., Loughman, T.: The CIO's chief concern: Communication. Inf. Manag. **27**(2), 129–137 (1994)
69. Štemberger, M.I., Manfreda, A., Kovačič, A.: Achieving top management support with business knowledge and role of IT/IS personnel. Int. J. Inf. Manag. **31**(5), 428–436 (2011)
70. Tan, F.B., Gallupe, R.B.: Aligning business and information systems thinking: a cognitive approach. IEEE Trans. Eng. Manag. **53**(2), 223–237 (2006)
71. Van de Ven, A.H., Walker, G.: The dynamics of interorganizational coordination. Adm. Sci. Q. **29**(4), 598–621 (1984)
72. Venkatesh, V., Brown, S.A., Bala, H.: Bridging the qualitative-quantitative divide: guidelines for conducting mixed methods research in information systems. MIS Q. **37**(1), 21–54 (2013)
73. Walsham, G.: Doing interpretive research. Eur. J. Inf. Syst. **15**(1), 320–330 (2006)
74. Watson, R.T.: Influences on the IS manager's perceptions of key issues: information scanning and the relationship with the CEO. MIS Q. **14**(2), 217–231 (1990)
75. Watts, S., Henderson, J.C.: Innovative IT climates: CIO perspectives. J. Strateg. Inf. Syst. **15**(2), 125–151 (2006)

Appendix A
The CIO/CEO Interview Guide

Part 1: General questions regarding the interviewee and interviewee's company

(1.1) Only CIO: What is your current position called?

(1.2) How many years have you been working in your current position? What position did you have before?

(1.3) Only CIO: Are you a member of the top management board? If not, at which management level do you work?

(1.4) Only CIO: To which manager do you report?

(1.5) Only CIO: Are you also responsible for other functions beside IT (e.g., organizational development)?

(1.6) What is the highest qualification you hold? In which area do you have this qualification?

(1.7) How do you define the term information technology (IT) in your company?

Part 2: Associations

(2.1) When you think about IT within your organization, what do you spontaneously associate with it? (max. five terms)

(2.2) When you think about the communication with your CEO/CIO, what do you spontaneously associate with it? (max. five terms)

Part 3: Main part

(3.1a) How do you rate the effectiveness of your communication with your CEO/CIO?

1	2	3	4	5	6	7
Completely problematic	Mostly problematic	Rather problematic	Moderate	Partly informative	Mostly informative	Fully informative

© The Author(s) 2017
A. Hütter et al., *On the Nature of Effective CIO/CEO Communication*,
SpringerBriefs in Information Systems, DOI 10.1007/978-3-319-50535-0

(3.1b) Please give an example that illustrates your point of view.
 (3.2) Do you communicate directly with your CEO/CIO about IT issues? If not, with whom do you communicate about them? If so, with who else do you communicate about it?
 (3.3) How often do you communicate with your CEO/CIO about IT issues during a typical month? How frequently should communication take place (in your opinion)?
 (3.4) Which communication channels do you use with your CEO/CIO (face-to-face, videoconference, telephone, e-mail, memo)? Please estimate their frequency of use (as a percentage).
 (3.5) About which IT topics do you communicate with your CEO/CIO?
 (3.6) What influences the effectiveness of the communication with the CEO/CIO from your point of view? What could be improved?
(3.7a) How do you rate the importance of IT for your business?

1	2	3	4	5	6	7
Completely unimportant	Largely unimportant	Rather unimportant	Indifferent	Partly a competitive factor	Largely a competitive factor	Fully a competitive factor

(3.7b) Please describe how IT supports the business areas and strategies of your company?
 (3.8) How would an IT breakdown affect the business activities of your company? In the short-term? In the long-term?
 (3.9) Please describe the contribution of IT to your business success (in your opinion)?
(3.10) How do you measure the performance of IT?
(3.11) Who decides whether an investment in IT is made or not? How is it decided?
(3.12) Only CEO: Do you participate in IT discussions about IT use within the organization? If so, how?
(3.13) Only CEO: How satisfied you are with the organization's IT?
(3.14) Only CEO: How strong was your influence on the selection of the CIO?

Part 4: Summary and conclusion

Have we forgotten something important? Do you have any questions? Thank you.

Appendix B
Detailed Information About the Interviews

Table B.1 provides detailed information about the CIO/CEO interviews and their transcripts length.

Table B.1 CIO/CEO interviews and transcripts length

Comp. ID	CIO interview length (h:m:s)	CIO transcript page length[a]	CEO interview length (h:m:s)	CEO transcript page length[a]
A	00:47:41	11.5	00:44:46	10.5
B	00:32:30	10.5	00:36:44	10.0
C	00:50:09	9.0	00:39:25	8.0
D	00:42:18	9.0	00:27:16	8.0
E	00:36:45	9.5	00:51:30	8.5
F	00:15:19	7.5	00:20:15	7.5
G	00:48:35	10.5	00:19:26	7.5
H	00:22:40	7.0	00:20:46	7.5
I	00:39:30	9.5	00:21:32	8.0
J	00:28:01	8.0	00:28:22	8.0
K	00:29:00	8.5	00:16:50	7.0
L	00:48:44	7.5	00:16:05	7.5
Sum	7:21:12	108.0	5:42:57	98.0

[a]We use the font Arial with size of 11 points and line spacing at 1.5 for all transcripts

© The Author(s) 2017
A. Hütter et al., *On the Nature of Effective CIO/CEO Communication*,
SpringerBriefs in Information Systems, DOI 10.1007/978-3-319-50535-0

Appendix C
Categorization Process

The categorization of CIO/CEO communication effectivity was based primarily on a CIO/CEO pair's responses to Question 3.1a (the seven-point scale about communication effectivity) and Question 3.1b (the example that should illustrate an interviewee's rating of communication effectivity). To further validate the reported level of effectivity, we analyzed what terms a CIO/CEO pair associate with their communication (Question 2.2), and reviewed their answers to open-end questions about communication. In cases where a CIO/CEO pair rated their communication effectivity high, but expressed major reservations or unfavorable contrasts with their communication, we downgraded their reported level of effectivity and vice versa. Table C.1 summarizes the interviewee responses to Questions 3.1a and 2.2, as well as our final rating of CIO/CEO communication effectivity.

The categorization of the shared CIO/CEO understanding of role of IT was based primarily on a CIO/CEO pair's responses to Question 3.7a (the seven-point scale about the business importance of IT) and Question 3.7b (the description about how IT supports the business areas and strategies). To further validate the initially classified level of shared understanding, we analyzed what terms a CIO/CEO pair associates with the IT in their company (Question 2.1), and reviewed their answers to open-end questions about IT. In cases where a CIO/CEO reported major differences about IT, we downgraded their level of shared understanding and vice versa. Table C.2 summarizes the interviewee responses to Question 3.7a and 2.1, as well as our final rating of the shared CIO/CEO understanding of the role of IT.

© The Author(s) 2017
A. Hütter et al., *On the Nature of Effective CIO/CEO Communication*,
SpringerBriefs in Information Systems, DOI 10.1007/978-3-319-50535-0

Table C.1 Categorization of the CIO/CEO communication effectivity

Comp. ID	CIO rating of communication effectivity with the CEO[a]	CIO associations with the CEO communication	CEO rating of communication effectivity with the CIO[a]	CEO associations with the CIO communication	Effectivity of CIO/CEO communication
A	6—Mostly informative	Consultative, uncomplicated, experienced, does not interfere	7—Fully informative	Regular meetings, IT steering committee, IT requests, steering committee meetings for large projects, budget overruns	High
B	6—Mostly informative	Little time, structured, at the same level, information flow in both directions	6—Mostly informative	Openness, lot of trust, good leadership skills, sometimes not so professional as he should be	Medium-high
C	6—Mostly informative	Good basis for discussion, listens to my wishes and needs, ability to develop new topics on my own, open for new topics, plenty of scope	6—Mostly informative	I have to advise the CIO, CIO has a difficult job, has a positive laid back attitude, good communication	Medium
D	6—Mostly informative	Strategic unison, goal orientation, persuasion, opinion formation	6—Mostly informative	Tension between past IT approach and new requirements, project meetings, capacity issues, cost issues, too little discussion about the requirements of current business operations	Medium-high
E	7—Fully informative	Open communication, short distance, quick decision-making	7—Fully informative	Budget, cost, organizational development, support for improvements in business areas	High
F	7—Fully informative	Direct, companionable, contact person because he used to be the head of IT	7—Fully informative	Data preparation, data analysis, user support, communication with external service providers	High

(continued)

Table C.1 (continued)

Comp. ID	CIO rating of communication effectivity with the CEO[a]	CIO associations with the CEO communication	CEO rating of communication effectivity with the CIO[a]	CEO associations with the CIO communication	Effectivity of CIO/CEO communication
G	6—Mostly informative	Amicable, understanding, definitely interested, reduced to key topics, not intensive communication but enough	6—Mostly informative	Know-how, value-added, helicopter perspective	Medium-high
H	4—Indifferent	Time pressure, too little, justification	4—Indifferent	Data security, dependence on IT staff, state of the art technology	Low
I	5—Partly informative	Too little, too cost-driven, but willingness for innovation, discussions about flexibility, shared understanding of strategy	6—Mostly informative	Open, honest, transparent, comprehensive, politically correct	Medium-high
J	7—Fully informative	Open, straightforward, at any time, always listens to my wishes and needs, courteous	6—Mostly informative	Event-driven, open, sparse	Medium-high
K	6—Mostly informative	Agreement about current activities, strategy coordination, budget coordination, coordination of project contents, general perspective of IT	6—Mostly informative	Regular exchange	Medium-high
L	6—Mostly informative	Regular meeting, shared vision and understanding, constructive, pleasant	6—Mostly informative	Regular, calm, very interested, years of experience, conservative	High

[a]CIOs/CEOs rated on a scale of 1 (completely problematic) to 7 (fully informative) how effectively they communicate about IT issues

Table C.2 Categorization of shared CIO/CEO understanding of the role of IT

Comp. ID	CIO rating of business importance of IT[a]	CIO associations with IT in the organization	CEO rating of business importance of IT[a]	CEO associations with the IT in the organization	Shared CIO/CEO understanding of the role of IT
A	5—Partly a competitive factor	Outsourcing, cutting costs, enables processes, monitoring technology market, security	5—Partly a competitive factor	Solution-oriented, competent, realizes large projects with external partner, discussing sometimes off-topic issues, basically positive	High
B	7—Fully a competitive factor	Risk, support of business processes, complexity, technology, knowledge	7—Fully a competitive factor	Organization, production means, data pool, committed IT staff, very central department	High
C	6—Largely a competitive factor	Flexibility, broad professional knowledge but not in depth, solution-oriented working style, good IT team, driver of innovation	5—Partly a competitive factor	Hardware, frontend, printer problems, SAP, applications	Low-medium
D	7—Fully a competitive factor	Structure, processes, consulting, support, areas of tension	6—Largely a competitive factor	Essential, important, ongoing investments, in need of reform, permanent challenge to stay up-to-date	Medium
E	6—Largely a competitive factor	Innovation, reliability, optimally adapted tools to the processes of employees, process support	7—Fully a competitive factor	Technology, organization, driver of innovation, important factor in the company, strategic implementations to be implemented based exclusively on IT	High
F	5—Partly a competitive factor	Forward-looking, essential, application software	6—Largely a competitive factor	Server, PCs, users, software, hardware	Medium-high

(continued)

Table C.2 (continued)

Comp. ID	CIO rating of business importance of IT[a]	CIO associations with IT in the organization	CEO rating of business importance of IT[a]	CEO associations with the IT in the organization	Shared CIO/CEO understanding of the role of IT
G	6—Largely a competitive factor	Analyzing, standardization, centralization, information availability, efficiency improvement	7—Fully a competitive factor	Information, storage, costs, value-added	Medium-high
H	6—Largely a competitive factor	Cost-intensive, difficult to manage, great opportunity, but also a risk	6—Largely a competitive factor	Facilitation, data security, education level of IT staff, security leaks	Medium
I	6—Largely a competitive factor	Technology, innovation, cost-center vs. profit center, shared service center approach, process optimization through IT	5—Partly a competitive factor	Less problems than in other business areas, poor support, complex process, administration, effectiveness	Medium-high
J	6—Largely a competitive factor	Network, service orientation, data center operations, security, mobile working	5—Partly a competitive factor	Pragmatic, helpful, lean, competent	Medium-high
K	6—Largely a competitive factor	Business enabler, supports core processes, applications, infrastructure, data center operations	6—Largely a competitive factor	Very advanced, important for the company, costs money	Medium-high
L	6—Largely a competitive factor	Service provider, cost-conscious, business enabler, process companion	7—Fully a competitive factor	Reliability, conservative, years of experience, following technology rather than leading, security	High

[a]CIOs/CEOs rated how important IT is for their business on a scale of 1 (completely unimportant) to 7 (fully a competitive factor)